COMMON THREAD:
THE SONGS OF THE EAGLES

Album Art Direction and Embroidery: Gabrielle Raumberger
Design: Gabrielle Raumberger & Dylan Tran
Photography: (Front Cover): Doris Ulmann (1882-1934), from the Doris Ulmann Collection,
#1346, courtesy of Special Collections, University of Oregon Library, part of her series
on the people of the Appalachians, c. 1920
Photography: (Background): Victor Bracke

C O N T E N T S

TAKE IT EASY

Words and Music by
JACKSON BROWNE and GLENN FREY

Moderate Country feeling

Well, I'm a - run-nin' down the road try'n' to loos-en my load,__ I've got sev-en wom-en on my__ mind, four__ that wan-na own me,__ two__ that wan-na stone me,__ one__ says she's a friend__ of mine.__

6

Peaceful Easy Feeling

Words and Music by
JACK TEMPCHIN

DESPERADO

**Words and Music by
DON HENLEY and GLENN FREY**

Slowly

Des - per - a - do,   *why don't__ you come to your sens - es?*   *You been out rid - in' fenc - es for*

HEARTACHE TONIGHT

Words and Music by
DON HENLEY, GLENN FREY,
BOB SEGER and JOHN DAVID SOUTHER

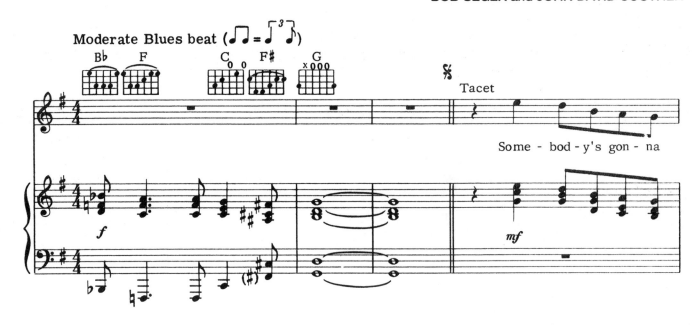

Let's go. _____ We can beat a-round the bush-es; we can

get down to the bone; we can leave it in the park-in' lot, but ei-ther way, there's gon-na be a

heart-ache to-night, ____ a heart-ache to-night, I know. ____ Oh, I

know. ___ There'll be a heart - ache to-night, ___ a heart-ache to-night, I know. ___

TEQUILA SUNRISE

Words and Music by
DON HENLEY and GLENN FREY

It's an-oth-er te-qui-la sun-rise star-in' slow-ly 'cross the sky, said good-bye.

TAKE IT TO THE LIMIT

Words and Music by
DON HENLEY,
GLENN FREY and RANDY MEISNER

I CAN'T TELL YOU WHY

Words and Music by
DON HENLEY,
GLENN FREY and TIMOTHY B. SCHMIT

LYIN' EYES

Words and Music by
DON HENLEY and GLENN FREY

NEW KID IN TOWN

Words and Music by
DON HENLEY,
GLENN FREY and JOHN DAVID SOUTHER

Moderately

There's talk on the street;_ it sounds so fa-mil - iar.
You look in her eyes;_ the mu - sic be-gins to play.

John-ny-come-late - ly, the new kid in town.
John-ny-come-late - ly, the new kid in town.

Ev-'ry-bod-y loves you, so don't let them down.
Will she still love you

when you're not a - round?

There's so man-y things you should have told her,

SATURDAY NIGHT

Words and Music by
RANDY MEISNER, DON HENLEY,
GLENN FREY and BERNIE LEADON

Seems like a dream now, it was so long a-go, the moon burned so bright and the time went so slow. And I

ALREADY GONE

Words and Music by
JACK TEMPCHIN and ROBB STRANDLUND

THE BEST OF MY LOVE

Words and Music by
DON HENLEY,
GLENN FREY and JOHN DAVID SOUTHER

THE SAD CAFE

Words and Music by
DON HENLEY, GLENN FREY,
JOE WALSH and J.D. SOUTHER

Out _____ in the shin - y night, _____ the
Oh, it seemed like a ho - ly place, _____ pro - te-
May - be the time _____ has drawn _____ the

rain was soft - ly fall - ing.
tect - ed by _____ a - maz - ing grace. _____
fac - es I _____ re - call. _____

And I re-mem-ber the times we spent in in-
We were part of the lone-ly crowd in in-
So meet me at mid-night, babe, in-

side the Sad Ca-fé.
side the Sad Ca-fé.
side the Sad Ca-fé.

Oh, ex-pect-ing to fly, we would

meet on that beau-ti-ful shore in the sweet by-and-by.